Thankyou for purchasing
The Roller Derby Coloui

I've been skating Derby for nearly 5 years. It has given me
so much back for every bruise I've put in. I love this crazy
sport and I'm always excited to illustrate the Roller Derby
world. I created this book to celebrate all of you.

So, get your pencils sharpened and get ready to dive in! You'll
find the book has blank pages on the back of the illustrations
so that any bleed through will not ruin your masterpieces. It
also means you can cut out your favourites for display
without losing any pages- so show them off!

I'd love to see what you create. You can find me online at:

twitter.com/shonapenny
or
facebook.com/shonapennyart

Happy Colouring!

Shona "Sho Time" Penny

DERBY MERIT BADGES

Design a Bruise!

1. The "...ne Nebula"

2. The "..."

3. The "Crescent Moon"

4. The "Purple Heart"

Made in the USA
San Bernardino, CA
23 November 2019